Sara
Franceys

Testament of Job

In Modern English
And Original Translation

Also by Pauly Hart

By the Gates of the Garden of Eden
Superior Respondent
Ouesso to Epena
The Book of Lesser Voices
Sometimes I Write Tiny Stories
Adelphoi
Stupid Mind Tricks
Book of Love and Laughter
The Cross and the Poet
What is Poep?
I Love You More Than a Fox Loves Blueberries
The Night Clerk Held a Broken Pencil
Spontaneous Psalms
Kick the Prick
My Flat Earth
Biblical Cosmology
Mathmagician and Other Tales of Awesomeness
The Richest Man in Babylon Continued Stories

(Periodicals)
Modern Epistle
Microzine

(With children authors)
Farrell Family Fables

(With Co-Author Jennifer Hart)
Adulting: A Daily Guide on Being an Adultier Adult

Testament of Job

In Modern English
And Original Translation

By Pauly Hart

And M.R. James

ISBN: 978-1-955399-02-9

Library of Congress Catalog Data is available at: Loc.gov
This book is available at cost on Amazon.com and wherever fine books are sold.

Any references to historical events, real people, or real places are used fictitiously. Names, characters, and places are products of the author's imagination.

Front cover art: William Blake, "Job's Sons and Daughters Overwhelmed by Satan," 1818
Front cover design by Pauly Hart

Paperback version printed in Savannah, Georgia, USA, where available.

First Edition, 2021
Author Contact: EmpiresAndGenerals@gmail.com
Author Website: PaulyHart.com

For
Erin Doom,
Rob, and Noel

Preface

It was late on Thursday night and the virtual "Bible Study" was off and running again, without a hitch. Hank was there, saying hi to everyone, and it was going swimmingly. We were studying "Job" and I was thrilled. But wait. This didn't sound like the Job I remembered. Wait a minute. This wasn't the Bible, it was something else.

What was going on here? Was my Bible broken again? Had I not noticed another book, lurking in the shadows between "Maps" and "Index?" No. Nothing was askew; it was just another book that they never put into the bible. That seemed odd. "Why was that?" I wondered. So I've been hunting, trying to figure out what this book is, and if there are more of them. Well, there are certainly a lot of them. Almost as many books as the whole of the Protestant Canon... That is: Genesis to Revelation.

The Roman Catholic Canon includes something called the "Deuterocanon" or "Apocryphal" scripts and there are 15 of those, and the Ethiopian Orthodox Church has even included books like Jubilees and 1st Enoch. Wow. I thought there were only 70 books (Psalms being 5 books – not the 66 I thought they were growing up in Sunday School). There are 1st – 4th Maccabees, The Letter of Jeremiah, Sirach, Odes, and others that I don't even know about.

So what is the actual Bible? Who told me it's only 70 books? Why can't I get an answer from God on this one? I don't know. All I know is there's a lot to sort through and you really have to rely on the Living Holy Spirit inside of you. He is a comforter and teaches us all things (John 14:26, 1 John 2:27). So, hey, Lord, please send Him into my mind to help me figure this stuff out!

Well, maybe He's already giving me wisdom. See, a lot of these texts are pseudepigrapha, meaning that someone wrote them and signed them with another person's name. 2nd and 3rd Enoch are probably this way. As a matter of fact, there's no doubt on those two. But just because it's a pseudepigrapha doesn't make it a false witness. Let's just say that if Aaron or Hur or Joshua helped old Moses write some of the stuff in the Pentateuch, we wouldn't call it a lie. As a matter of fact, we do know that Moses had a little help writing those 5 books, because at the end of Deuteronomy, Moses is dead! Someone had to finish it.

So a pseudepigraphal can be honored by God. I'm sure that Isaiah had a little help writing his work when he was hanging out with Hezekiah. There are countless other references, but for the most part, it's not an evil practice to do so. Let's just say it plainly. All forgeries are pseudepigrapha, but not all pseudepigrapha are forgeries.

When the Canon was first established they had five basic things they looked at.

Divine Inspired
Prophetic
Dynamic
Authentic
Having Testimony
In Agreement

I could write a book on how Canon was chosen in and of itself. The council of Jamnia, Trent, Worms, are all fun studies but I'm not going to subject you to that type of study at this time. Seriously, you would get so bored you might start to hate me a little.

We know that The "Testament of Job" was indeed pseudepigrapha as it was written sometime during the Second

Temple Period, and most assuredly not by Job. But as Martin Luther says about these books, "[they are] useful and good to read." So, I know it sounds trite, but if Luther said it, that's good enough for me. I mean, not really maybe, but I believe you get the point. I enjoy reading Josephus, I enjoy reading Polycarp, Clement, Justin Martyr, Tertullian, and Origin. They're good people and had interesting things to say. Except Augustine. That guy was a heretic. But I digress...

Hey, I love some of that stuff but it's not scripture.

The Testament of Job (this book) is not scripture.

It's just a great resource. A lot of them are really interesting and nice in tidbits to help you understand the world they lived in.

The Pilgrim's Progress, or The Screwtape Letters, or This Present Darkness, or The Lion, the Witch, and the Wardrobe are all fun books...

But they aren't scripture.

Again, let me tell you again...

This book is not scripture.

But it just might help you wrap your head around cool ideas that you wanted to explore a little more in your free time. I think it's awesome. I love writing, and I love writing good fiction. I might as well write "The Second Testament of Job" because it's a cool idea. What if I set it during the time that he got everything back and his second set of children were growing up? That might sell.

See what I mean? No one is going to pull out that novel on Sunday Morning Service. "Turn to page 109 and we will read about how Job bought some corn at the market." Nope. Not gonna happen... But, hey, if it does, you probably shouldn't be going to that church. That's just a weird church. Stick to the Word of God. Stick to The Bible.

And sure, there's plenty of the actual Bible to read without getting bored. Instead of Game of Thrones, maybe you should read "Bel and the Dragon" – cause, hey. Dragons are cool. J.R.R. Tolkien didn't invent them... Our Father in Heaven did.

At any rate, I hope you really enjoy this fun read.

-Pauly Hart
July, 2021

Introduction

"Testament of Job the Blameless
The Conqueror in Many Contests, the Sainted"

Later retitled:

"The Book of Job Called Jobab, and His Life,
And the Transcript of His Testament"

Now simply known as "Testament of Job," this book was written somewhere around the time of Christ, ranging from the first century BC to the first century AD. It is not clear when it was penned, but the earliest copy found was a manuscript in Coptic, dating around the 5th century, AD. Surviving copies have also been found in Greek and Slavonic.

The testament that you now have isn't anything to change your theology over. It's a story, maybe somewhat important in understanding the mind of Job, through the original author's pen... Or quill... Or chisel. But it's a story nonetheless about a man named Job, the same one that we read about in "The Book of Job" which is part of the authorized canon of both Jewish and Christian faiths.

There are some distinct similarities in this book to the above mentioned, and there are some glaring differences. Yes, Job is tempted and put through trials by Satan. But the Satan that appears in this book is of more evil intent. The Satan that appears in the original book is a type of lawyer, a type of schoolmaster, daring Yahway Elohim to prove how much his creations love Him.

The Satan presented here is a horrible and malfeasant fellow, bent on the complete annihilation of Job, as much as

Yahway will allow it. In the original book, Job is stripped of everything, in this book, he retains some key possessions, namely, his ruling crown. In the original book, his first wife is seen as a shrew, in this one, more honor is given to her. She is the picture of a seven years of hard patience. But eventually, both in the original and in this book, her patience comes to an end with the most famous words: "Curse God and die."

There is also importance and a large distinction given between the attitudes of the three friends in the original and their attitude here. In this work, they are angry often and ready to give up at a moment's notice. There is also a glaring lack of discourse in this work, which is the meat of the original book. Perhaps the writer of this work felt nothing really new needed to be said.

Job's attitude in this book is also strikingly different than the first. In this book, there is a messianic prophesy and a joy that knows no end, compared to there is a sense of morose fatigue that he must endure to the end. Little concentration is given over to the ethics of the first book, but some remains of the idea that we are not The Creator and only He knows how the world really works and how we should function within it.

Elihu is judged much more harshly and, though his discourse is missing purposefully, there is a stern judgement against him, as he allows Satan to enter into his mind and speak through him. There is a dirge for Elihu, a lament of his fallen nature. Job is seen as the ultimate hero, withstanding even the vile speech from his youngest friend.

At the end of the book, there is a stark departure from the original text and we have a side story about three (no, four) angelic ropes, or girdles. These seemingly blessed and magical talisman's allow Job's newest three daughters to speak in the otherworldly tongues of Angels, Archons, and Cherubim. This is an eye opening account of "Speaking in tongues" as it not only allows them to compose hymns in this new language, but keeps them (and their breasts) pure and free from defilement.

Some consideration for this ending story is needed. Around the time of Hesiod and Homer, there were the three Graeae, the gray witches who divined and shared one eye between them. I do not think the writer is borrowing from this material because there is nothing similar in their cases, save the number of them to be three. I can only think that this is an original creation of the writer, but it is unknown why he included this reference. Many translators of the text have sought to delete it, but it remains here.

The writing style is that of first person, as though Job tells us the story himself. We know from studying the patriarchs that the tradition is to have a family member, usually the closest remaining male relative, write their story from their deathbed. At the end of the work, the writing changes from the first person telling of Job, to that of his brother, Nahor. His brother picks up the pen and finishes Job's story, and that of his three daughters.

Overall I find The Testament of Job beneficial in the believer's life. Even if approached from a classical aspect, this book tells of the never-ending mercies of The Benevolent Creator, and though He may allow us to be tested, His love endures and He rewards those who seek Him.

For the Israelite, this book serves as a historical reminder that though we may expound on Scripture, Hashem remains the writer of the story of our lives. For the Christian, this book serves as a marker of faith for those who trust in their God. For both, it serves as a story rooted in the life of a Patriarch, the man and King named Job. That we can take away from this the lessons found therein is a hope that one might have for all reading. That it features one of the most well-known characters in history, is a testament, aside from this one, of the man himself.

I pray you find this testament comforting, knowing that God cares for His children. As Job's first wife said, before death: "Now I know that Yahway remembers me."

Testament of Job

In Modern English

1

1 On the day Jobab became sick, he knew that he would have to leave his house. He called his seven sons and his three daughters together and spoke to them saying:

2 "Form a circle around me, children, and listen, and I will tell you what Yahuah did for me and all that happened to me.

3 I am Job your father.

4 Listen to me children. Know that you are the generation of the chosen one, so take heed of your noble birth.

5 I am the son of Esau, brother of Nahor. Your mother is Dinah. By her have I become your father.

6 My first wife died with my other ten children in bitter death.

7 Listen children, and I will reveal unto you what happened to me.

8 I was a very rich man living east in the land of Uz, and before Yahuah had named me Job, I was called Jobab.

9 The beginning of my trial started this way: Near my house there was the idol of one worshipped by the people. I always saw burned offerings brought to it as an elohim.

10 Then I pondered and said to myself: "Is this He who made heaven, earth, sea, and men? How am I to know the truth?"

11 And in that night as I lay asleep, a voice came and called: "Jobab! Jobab! Rise up, and I'll tell you about the one you asked about. I will tell you who he is."

12 The people who bring burned offerings to this idol, they should know it is not Elohim. It is the power and work of Satan by which he beguiles these people."

13 When I heard this, I fell upon the earth and I prostrated myself saying:

14 "My Adonai, who speaks for the salvation of my soul. I pray to you, if this is the idol of Satan, I pray to you, let me go now and destroy it and purify this spot.

15 There is nobody that can stop me doing this. I am the king of this land, so that those that live in it will no longer be led astray."

16 And the voice that spoke out of the flame answered to me: "You may purify this spot.

17 But look, I announce to you what Yahuah ordered me to tell you, for I am the archangel of the Elohim."

18 And I said: "Whatever will be told to his servant. I will hear."

19 And the archangel said to me: "Yahuah speaks! 'If you destroy and takes away the image of Satan, he will set himself with wrath to wage war against you. Satan will use all his malice against you.

20 He will bring upon you many severe plagues, and take from you all that you have.

21 He will take away your children and will inflict many evils upon you.

22 Then you must wrestle like an athlete and resist pain. You must be sure of your reward, and overcome trials and afflictions.

23 But when you endure - I will make your name great throughout all generations of the earth unto the end of the world.

24 And I will restore to you all that you have. The double part of what you will lose will be given back to you. This is so you will know that Elohim does not consider the person but gives to each who deserves goodness.

25 And goodness will also be given to you and you will put on a crown of Amarant.

26 And at the resurrection you will wake for eternal life. Then you will know that Yahuah is just, and true and mighty."

27 I replied: "It's for the love of Elohim that I will endure until death everything that will come upon me. I will not shrink back."

28 Then the angel put his seal on me and left.

2

1 After this I got up in the night and took fifty of my workers. We went to the temple of the idol and demolished it down to the ground.

2 Then I went back to my house and gave orders that the door should be firmly locked; saying to my doorkeepers:

3 "If someone will ask for me, don't tell me, but tell him: He is looking into other important things. He is inside."

4 Then Satan disguised himself as a beggar and knocked loudly on the door, saying to the doorkeeper:

5 "Tell Job that I want to talk to him."

6 And the doorkeeper came in and told me, but I told the doorkeeper that I was studying.

7 The evil one failed. Then he put an broken basket on his shoulder and went in and spoke to the doorkeeper. "Tell Job: Give me bread from your hands so I can eat."

8 And when I heard this, I gave her burnt bread to give to him, and told him: "Don't expect to eat my bread, because it's forbidden."

9 But the doorkeeper was ashamed to hand him the ashy burnt bread. She took of her own bread and gave it to him, because she didn't know it was Satan.

10 Knowing what happened, he took it and spoke to the young woman. "Go away bad servant, and bring me the bread that was given to you to hand to me."

11 And the servant cried and spoke sadly. "You're telling the truth, saying that I am a bad servant because I have not done as I was told by my master."

12 She turned back and brought him the burnt bread. "My Adonai says: "You will not eat of my bread anymore, it's forbidden."

13 But he sent it back to me and I said: "I'll give this in order that the charge may not be brought against me. I give to the enemy who asked."

14 When Satan heard this, he sent back the doorkeeper to me. "As you see this bread all burnt, and I will soon burn your body to make it just like this."

15 I replied: "Do whatever you want and do whatever you plot. I am ready to endure whatever you bring upon me."

16 When the devil heard this, he left. He walked up under the highest heaven, and he took from Yahuah a promise. The promise that he might have power over all my possessions.

17 After taking the power to do this, he went away and instantly took all my wealth.

3

1 I had one hundred and thirty thousand sheep. I used seven thousand for the clothing of orphans and widows and of needy and sick ones.

2 I had a herd of eight hundred dogs who watched my sheep and besides these two hundred to watch my house.

3 And I had nine mills working for the whole city and ships to carry goods. I placed them in every city and into the villages to the feeble and sick and to those that were unfortunate.

4 I had three hundred and forty thousand wild donkeys. From these I set aside five hundred and their kids. I ordered them to be sold and the proceeds to be given to the poor and the needy.

5 For from all the lands the poor came to meet me.

6 The four doors of my house were opened. Each had a watchman who looked to see whether there were any people coming asking alms. When they would see me sitting at one of the doors, they could take what they needed and leave through any other door.

7 I also had thirty immovable tables set at all hours for strangers. I also had twelve tables spread for the widows.

8 If any one came asking for alms, he found food on my table to take all he needed. I turned nobody away to leave my door with an empty stomach.

9 I also had three thousand five hundred yokes of oxen. I selected from them five hundred and had them tend to the plowing.

10 And with these I did all the work in each field by those who would do it. I took in the labor and the income of their crops I laid aside for the poor on their table.

11 I also had fifty bakeries from which I sent the bread to the table for the poor.

12 And I had workers selected for this service.

13 There were also some strangers who saw my good will; they wished to serve as deacons themselves.

14 Others, being in distress and unable to make a living, came with the request saying:

15 "Sir, we beg you, since we can also fill this office of deacons and have no possessions. Have pity upon us and advance money to us in order that we may go into the great cities and sell merchandise.

16 And the excess of our profits we will also give to help the poor, and then we will return to your money back to you.

17 And when I heard this, I was glad that they would take this work for the love of the poor.

18 So with a willing heart I gave them what they wanted. I signed their contracts, but would not take any other security from them except their word.

19 And they went abroad and gave to the poor and they were successful.

20 Frequently, some of their goods were lost on the road or on the sea, or they were robbed.

21 They would come and say: "We beg you, act kindly to us in order that we may figure out how we can restore to you what was yours."

22 When I heard this, I had sympathy with them. I found their contract; I would read it and then tear it up, releasing them of the debt, saying to them:

23 "What I have set apart for the poor, I will not take from you".

24 So I accepted nothing from those who owed me.

25 Once, a man with a cheerful heart came to me and said: "I don't need to be compelled to be a paid worker for the poor.

26 But I still wish to serve the needy at your table." So he agreed to work, and he ate his share.

27 I gave him his wages anyway, and I went home happy.

28 But when he didn't want to take it, I forced him to. I told him: "I know you're a working man who looks for and waits for his wages, and you must take it."

29 I never put off paying the wages of anyone that I hired. I never kept in my house anything from a laborer, not even for an evening, if I owed him.

30 Those that milked the cows and the sheep waved to those walking by that they should take their share of the milk.

31 For the milk flowed in such plenty that it curdled into butter on the hills and by the roadside. It also went by the rocks and the hills the cattle where lay which had given birth to their offspring.

32 But my workers grew weary feeding the widows and the poor and dividing it into small pieces.

33 They would curse me and say: "If we just had his flesh we would be satisfied," even though I was very kind to them,

34 I also had six harps and six workers to play the harps and also a cithara, and other stringed instruments, and I strummed it during the day.

35 And I took the cithara, and played it for the widows, after their meals.

36 And with the instrument I reminded them of Elohim that they should give praise to Yahuah.

37 And when my musicians would murmur, I took the musical instruments and played as much as they would have done for their wages. I did this to give them a break from their work.

4

1 My children took care of the service. Then they took their meals each day along with their three sisters beginning with the older brother, and made a feast.

2 I rose in the morning and offered a sin-offering for them: fifty rams and nineteen sheep. What remained from the sacrifice, I gave to the poor.

3 And I said to the poor: "Take these left-overs and pray for my children.

4 Maybe my sons have sinned before Yahuah, speaking pridefully: 'We are children of this rich man. These are our things! Why should we be servants to the poor?'"

5 So in speaking pridefully this way, they may have provoked the anger of Elohim, for great pride is an offense before Yahuah."

6 So I brought cattle as an offering to the priest at the altar saying: "May my children never think evil towards Elohim in their hearts."

7 While I lived in this manner, the Seducer could not bear to see the good that I did, and he demanded the warfare of Elohim against me.

8 And he came upon me cruelly.

9 First he burned up the large herds of my sheep. Then the camels, then he burned up the cattle and all my herds. Either this or they were captured by my enemies and also by the people that I had helped.

10 The shepherds came and told me about it.

11 But when I heard it, I gave praise to Elohim and didn't curse Him.

12 And when the Seducer learned of my inner strength, he plotted new things against me.

13 He disguised himself as The King of Persia and sieged my city. After he had captured everyone that was in my house, he spoke to them with evil intent, saying pridefully:

14 "This man Job who has gotten all the goods of the earth and left nothing for others! He has destroyed and torn down the temple of Elohim.

15 So I'm going to repay him what he did to the house of the great Elohim.

16 Now come with me and we will steal and destroy everything that's left in his house."

17 And they answered and said to him: "He has seven sons and three daughters.

18 Be careful before they flee into other lands and they may become tyrants and come at us with force and kill us."

19 And he said: Don't be afraid at all. I destroyed his flocks and his money with fire. I captured everyone else, and I will kill his children."

20 Saying that, he threw open the house and killed my children.

21 And my subjects, seeing that what he said became true, chased me down, and robbed me of everything that was in my house.

22 I saw with my own eyes the destruction of my house. Men without culture and without honor sat at my table and on my couches, and I couldn't say anything against them.

23 I was as exhausted as a woman during menstrual pains. But I remembered that this warfare was spoken over me by Yahuah through His angel.

24 And I became like a ship captain, when looking at the rough sea and the cross winds. He knows that the weight of the ship in the middle of the ocean is too heavy, so he throws the cargo into the sea, and says:

25 "I have to destroy all my cargo so I can land safely at the city! At least I can sell the rescued ship and the best of my things."

26 So I managed my own affairs.

27 But then another messenger came and told me about the death of my own children, and I was shaken with fear.

28 And I tore my clothes and said:
"Yahuah hath given,
Yahuah hath taken.
As it seemed best to Yahuah,
So it has happened to be.
May the name of Yahuah be blessed."

5

1 Satan saw that he could not put me to shame. So he went and asked Yahuah permission to inflict plague on my body, for the Evil one could not bear my patience.

2 Then Yahuah delivered me into his hands to use my body as he wanted, but he gave him no power over my soul.

3 And he came to me as I was sitting on my throne still mourning over my children.

4 And he resembled a great hurricane and turned over my throne and threw me on the ground.

5 I continued lying on the floor for three hours. Then he smote me with a hard plague from the top of my head to the toes of my feet.

6 And I left the city in great distress and sadness came and sat down upon a dunghill. My body was being eaten by maggots.

7 And I wet the earth with the water from my sore body, for my flesh flowed off my body, and many worms covered it.

8 When a single worm crept off my body, I put it back. "Remain on the spot where you have been placed until He who hath sent you will order you to go somewhere else."

9 In this way, I survived for seven years, sitting on a dung-hill outside of the city while being covered with a plague.

10 I saw with my own eyes my dead children were carried by angels to the heavens.

11 And my poor wife, who, when I married her, had her own servants and bodyguards, brought low. I saw her hauling water like a slave in the house of a common man just so she could buy a little bread and bring it to me.

12 And in my sickness I said: "These rich city men, who I never even considered as rich as my shepherd dogs, hire my wife to be their servant."

13 So I found courage once again.

14 But then after this, they only paid her enough so that she was only able to feed herself.

15 But she took it and divided it between herself and me, saying sadly: "Poor me! For my husband can't even eat enough bread! And he can't even go to the market to beg bread from the bread-sellers to bring it to me that we may both eat"

16 And when Satan learned this, he disguised himself as a bread-seller. Then he made it seem like an accident that my wife met him and she asked him for bread thinking that he was that sort of man.

17 But Satan said to her: "Give me money, and then take whatever you want."

18 But she answered: "Where am I supposed to get money? Don't you know about my bad luck? If you have any pity, please show it to me. If you don't have any, then I'll prove it to you."

19 And he replied saying: "If you didn't deserve this misfortune, you wouldn't have suffered like this.

20 Now, if there's no money in your hand, then I'll buy the hair off of your head. I'll sell you three loaves of bread for it, so that you can at least live on it for three days."

21 Then she said to herself: "What is the hair of my head in comparison with my starving husband."

22 So after thinking about it, she said to him: "Rise and cut off my hair".

23 Then he took a pair of scissors and took off the hair of her head in the before everyone. Then he gave her three loaves of bread.

24 She took them and brought them to me. But Satan went behind her on the road, hiding himself as he walked and making her anxious.

6

1 Immediately my wife came near me and crying aloud and weeping she said: "Job! Job! How long will you sit upon the dung-hill outside the city, doing nothing but thinking about how you will be saved?

2 I have been wandering from place to place, working as hired servant, and no one even remembers you at all!

3 My sons and the daughters that I carried on my bosom are lost! The labors and pains that I've gone through have been for nothing!

4 And you sit in this foul smelling place covered with sores and maggots, sleeping in the cold!

5 I have gone through every trial and problem and pain, all day and night until I was able to bring bread to you.

6 They no longer give me any extra. I can barely take my own food and share it with you, but I thought it wasn't right that you should be in such pain and hunger.

7 And so I went to the market boldly. When the bread-seller told me: "Give me money and will have bread". I told him our problem.

8 Then he said: "If you don't have money, hand me your hair, and take three loaves of bread so that you can live three more days."

9 I knew it was wrong but had him do it anyway. "Get up and cut off my hair!" He got up and cut off my hair with the scissors in the middle of the market while the crowd looked on.

10 Who wouldn't be taken aback?
They say: "Is this Sitis,
The wife of King Job,
Who had fourteen curtains

To cover her dining room,
And doors within doors
So that when you visited her house,
Your breath was taken away.
And now she sells her hair for bread!

11 Who had camels laden with goods,
And they were brought
Into remote lands to the poor,
And now she sells her hair for bread!

12 Behold her who had seven tables
Immovably set in her house
At which each poor man
And each stranger ate,
And now she sells her hair for bread!

13 Behold her who had the basin
Wherewith to wash her feet
Made of gold and silver,
And now she walks upon the ground
And now she sells her hair for bread!

14 Behold her who had her garments
Made of byssus interwoven with gold,
And now she sells her hair for bread!

15 Behold her who had couches
Of gold and of silver,
And now she sells her hair for bread!"

16 Job, all these things were said to me, but I only have one thing to say to you:

17 "Since the weakness of my heart has made me so weary, get up, take these loaves of bread and enjoy them. Then speak against Yahuah and die!

18 I am ready to trade the laziness of death for the life of my body."

19 But I replied to her "Listen! For seven years I have been covered with the plague, and I have put up with the maggots! I haven't been put down by any of these things.

20 But about what you said: 'Speak against Elohim and die!' - We are in this together. We can make it through together.

21 But you want me to speak against Elohim and that He should be exchanged for the elohim of the land of the dead.

22 Why don't you remember all the good things we had? If these goods come from the lands of Yahuah, shouldn't we endure these evils? Shouldn't we have courage in everything until Yahuah has mercy again and shows pity on us?

23 Don't you see the Seducer standing behind you and confusing your thoughts so that you would trick me?

24 And he turned to Satan and said: "Why don't you openly try to stop me? Stop hiding yourself you horrible one.

25 Does the lion show his strength in a small cage? Or does a bird fly around inside of a basket? I'm telling you: Go away and wage your war against me."

26 Then he came out from behind my wife and placed himself before me. He cried loudly and said: "Oh listen Job! You win! I give up! You who are only flesh while I am a spirit.

27 Even though you're stricken with the plague, I am in greater trouble.

28 I'm like a wrestler trying to fight another wrestler! In single-handed combat he tore down his enemy, threw dirt on him, and broke his arms and legs! But what about the other guy - the loser who lies on the ground? He shouts to the world about how brave he is, and tells everyone what a great fight it was.

29 It's you, Job! You're the one beneath! You're covered in plague and pain but it's you who actually took the victory in the wrestling match! I yield!

30 Then in shame, he left.

31 Now my children, show a firm heart in all the evil that happens to you, for firmness of heart is greater than all things.

7

1 Around this time the kings heard what had happened to me and they got up and came to me. They came from their own lands to visit me and to comfort me.

2 And when they came near, they cried loudly and each king tore his clothes.

3 They bowed down and touched the earth with their heads, they sat down next to me for seven days and seven nights. Nobody spoke a word.

4 There were four of them: Eliphaz, the King of Teman, King Bilad, King Zophar, and also Elihu.

5 When they sat down, they talked about what had happened to me.

6 When they came to me at the beginning and I had shown them my precious stones, they were astonished and said:

7 "Even if all four of us pooled our resources it wouldn't equal the might of your kingdom, by the jewels in your

crown. You have greater nobility than all the people in the East."

8 And when, they had come to the land of Uz to visit me, they asked in the city: "Where is Jobab, the ruler of this whole land?"

9 And the men in the city told them about me: "He sits upon the dung-hill outside of the city. He has not entered the city for seven years".

10 And then they asked about all my things, and the men told the kings what had happened.

11 When they heard about me, they went out of the city with my fellow-citizens. They pointed me out to them.

12 They rebuked them and said: "This is not Jobab".

13 When they hesitated, Eliphaz, the King of Teman, said: "Let's get closer and see."

14 And when they came closer I remembered who they were, and I cried a lot when I learned why they came.

15 And I threw earth upon my head, and shook it, telling them that I was the man they looked for.

16 And when they saw me shake my head, they threw themselves down upon the ground, overcome with emotion.

17 The men from the city were stood around and the three kings lay down on the ground for three hours like dead men.

18 Then they got up and said to each other: We cannot believe that this is Jobab".

19 So for seven days they looked around and asked everyone questions. They searched for all my flocks and my belongings, but then they said:

20 "We know how much he sent to the poor villages that surrounded his house. We know how much he gave to the poor and we know how well he treated his own workers. How is it possible for him to have been brought this low to such a state of shame?"

21 So then after seven days Elihu said to the kings : "Let's get closer and examine him, whether he is Jobab or not."

22 They were about a half of a mile away from his stinky body. They got up and got closer and carryed perfume in their hands. Their soldiers went with them and threw fragrant incense all around them so that they could bear to come closer.

23 After three hours went by, covering the stink, they came to me.

24 Eliphaz began: "Are you really our fellow king Job? Are you really the one who used to be so glorious?

25 Are you the one who once shone like the sun on the whole earth? Are you the man who once resembled the moon and stars, so brilliant through the night?

26 I answered him and said: "I am." They all cried and were sorry, and they sang the royal song of lamentation. Their whole army joined them in the chorus.

27 Then Eliphaz asked me:
 "Are you he who had ordered

Seven thousand sheep to be given
For the clothing of the poor
Whither, then hath gone the glory of thy throne?

28 Are you the man who ordered
Three thousand cattle
To do the plowing
Of the field for the poor
Whither, then hath thy glory gone?

29 Are you the man who had golden couches,
And now you sit upon a dunghill
Whither then hath thy glory gone?

30 Are you the man who had sixty tables
Set for the poor
Are you the man who had censers

For the fine perfume
Made of precious stones
Here you are in a malodorous state
Whither then hath thy glory gone?

31 Are you the man who had golden candelabras
Set upon silver stands;
And now must you long
For the natural gleam of the moon
Whither then hath thy glory gone?

32 Are you the man
Who had ointment made
Of the spices of frankincense
And you sit in a state of ruin!
Whither then hath thy glory gone?

33 Are you the man who laughed
At the wrong doers and mock sinners
And now you have become
A laughingstock to all
Whither then hath thine glory gone?

34 And when Eliphaz had cried for a long time and was
sad, all the others joined him, so that the noise was very
great. Then I said to them:

35 "Be quiet and I will show you my throne, and the glory
of its splendor: For my glory will be eternal.

36 The whole world will be destroyed, and its glory will disappear. All those who hold onto it will stay low. My throne is in the upper world and its glory and shining light will be at the right of the Savior in the heavens.

37 My throne exists in the life of the holy ones and its glory in the world that can't be destroyed.

38 The rivers will be dry and their pride will go down to the dark pit! The rivers in my land in which my throne is, will never dry up, but will remain forever strong.

39 The kings and the rulers will disappear. Their glory and pride is like a reflection in a mirror... But my Kingdom lasts forever and ever, its glory and beauty is in the chariot of my Father.

8

1 When I spoke this way to them, Eliphaz became angry and told my other friends "Why did we even come and comfort Job? Listen! He tells us how wrong we are. Let's go back home.

2 This man sits here in misery worm-eaten in the middle of an unbearable stink, and then he challenges us? 'Kingdoms and rulers will fall, but my kingdom will last forever.' He says."

3 Then Eliphaz was angry and got up in a huff. He turned away from me and said angrily: "I'm leaving. Here we came to comfort him but now he declares war against us in front of our own armies!"

4 But Bildad seized Eliphaz by the hand and said:" Wait! We shouldn't speak this way to man in such a state, especially to one brought so low with so many troubles.

5 Listen! We are in good health, but didn't come near him because he stank so much, except with the help of plenty of perfumes. Eliphaz, you forget all this.

6 Let me speak plainly. Let's be forgiving and learn how he came to be like this. Maybe if he remembers how he used to be, he won't be driven crazy.

7 Who wouldn't be puzzled seeing him this way, enduring so many trials? Let me go a little closer so I can find out why he's this way.

8 Bildad got up and approached me saying: "Are you Job? Are you still full of courage?"

9 And I said: "I didn't hold fast to the stuff I owned, since the earth and everyone on it is always changing. But my hope lies in heaven, because there is no trouble there."

10 Bildad rejoined and said: "We know that the earth is always changing, it always changes every season. At times

earth is at peace, and at times it's at war. But heaven - we hear that it is perfectly steady.

11 Since you really are this calm, let me ask you a second question. Because, when you answered me the first time, you used encouraging words. So it appears that you really aren't crazy.

12 He said: "Upon what do you set your hope?"
And I said: "Upon the living Elohim."

13. He said: "Who robbed you of all your possessions? Who inflicted thee with these plagues?"
And I said: "Elohim."

14 He said: "If you still place your hope in Elohim, how can He do wrong in judgment? He brought on you plagues and misfortunes, and having taken from you all your possessions.

15 Since He took these, it is clear that He has given you nothing. No king will disgrace his soldier who has served him well as body-guard."

16 I answered: "Who understands the depths of Yahuah and of His wisdom to be able to accuse Elohim of injustice?"

17 So Bildad said: "Answer me this then, Job. If you are in such a state of wisdom, teach it to me.

18 Why do we see the sun rise in the East and set in the West, but in the morning we find the sun rising in the East? Tell me your thought about this."

19 So I said: "Why do I need to babble about the mighty mysteries of Elohim? What if I get it wrong when talking about things belonging to the Master? No, I won't do it!

20 Who are we that we should pry into matters about the heavens when we are only of flesh? No we're not even that. We're earth and ash!

21 I want you to know that I'm alright, so listen to what I ask you:

22 You eat food and drink water through the same throat. When you go and relieve yourself, they are back to two parts, solid and liquid, instead of one. How does that work?

23 Bildad said: "I don't know". So I said: "If can't even understand even the exits of the body, how can you understand the way the sky works?"

24 Then Zophar spoke up and said: "We're not asking about ourselves… We only want to know if you're alright. And from what we see, you seem like you know what you're doing.

25 So, now, what can we do for you? Look, we've come here, and brought the best doctors from our kingdoms so that they can cure you.

26 But I answered and said: "My cure comes from Elohim, the Maker of doctors".

9

1 And when I said this to them, my wife Sitis came running up to us, dressed in rags. She had come from working for her slave-owner, he had told her not to come, because the kings might capture her.

2 When she got there, she threw herself at their feet, crying and saying: "Remember me Eliphaz! Look at me! Remember how I was when I was with you, and see how I have changed! Look at these clothes!"

3 Then the kings started crying again, being astonished at not only Job, but his wife and then they were quiet. Eliphaz took his purple cape and threw it around her and wrapped her with it.

4 She said to Eliphaz: "I ask as favor of you, my lords, tell your soldiers to dig in the ruins of our house. There they will find my children. Get them so that we can bury them.

5 Because right now, because we are so abused, we have no energy to do it. The least you could do is help me see their bones.

6 I feel like a wild beast! Like the mother of a wild beasts. And that my ten children died and I couldn't even give them a decent burial."

7 Then the kings gave order that the ruins of my house should be dug up. But I stopped them and said:

8 "Don't go through the trouble! My children will not be found. They are in the presence of their Maker and Ruler."

9 But then the kings answered themselves: "Now who will deny that he is out of his mind and is babbling?

10 We want to bring the bones of his children back, but he stops us! He says: 'They have been taken and placed the keeping of their Maker.' Prove it!"

11 So I said: "Help me up so I can stand!" And they lifted me, holding up my arms from both sides.

12 And I stood up and before doing anything, I praised Elohim. After the prayer I said to them: "Look with your eyes to the East!"

13 And they looked and saw my children with crowns near the glory of the King, the Ruler of heaven.

14 When my wife Sitis saw it, she fell to the ground and bowed before Elohim, saying: "Now I know that Yahuah remembers me."

15 After she spoke, it was evening, she left us and went to the city, back to the master who she served as slave. She lay herself down in front of the cow manger and died of exhaustion.

16 When her evil master searched for her and didn't find her, he went to his herds. There he saw her stretched out upon the manger dead, while all the animals around were crying.

17 And all who saw her wept and lamented, and the cry extended throughout the whole city.

18 And the people brought her down and wrapped her up and buried her by the house which had fallen on her children.

19 And the poor of the city cried deeply for her and said: "Look, here is Sitis! There was never a more noble woman like her in glory! Oh woe is us! For now she can't even afford a proper tomb!"

20 Such was her death song that it was written down in the city records.

10

1 Eliphaz and those that were with him were astonished at these things. They sat down with me and replying to me, spoke in prideful words about me for twenty-seven days.

2 They repeated it again and again that I deserved the suffering for having done a lot of sins. They said there was no hope for me, but I argued in my defense.

3 And they got up in anger, ready to leave. But Elihu begged them to stay a little longer so he could show me what my sins were.

4 "We've been arguing with him for too many days, and he brags that he is innocent. I won't stand for it any longer.

5 Since we got here, I've cried over him, remembering how happy he used to be. But now he speaks so pridefully! He says that he has his throne in the heavens.

6 So listen! I'll tell you why things are the way they are."

7 Then, filled with Satan, Elihu spoke hard words which are not here, but are written down in the records left of Elihu.

8 After Elihu stopped, Elohim appeared to me in a storm and in clouds, and spoke. He blamed Elihu and showing

me that the voice of Elihu wasn't his own, but the voice of a wild beast.

9 And when Elohim had finished speaking to me, Yahuah spoke to Eliphaz: "You and your friends have sinned. You have not spoken the truth about my servant Job.

10 So get up and make him bring a sin-offering for you in order that your sins may be forgiven. Were it not for Job, I would have destroyed you."

11 So they brought to me all the things for a sacrifice. I took them and made a sin-offering for the kings, and Yahuah received it and forgave them for their sins.

12 Eliphaz, Bildad and Zophar saw that Elohim had pardoned their sin through His servant Job. When they saw that He didn't pardon Elihu, then Eliphaz begin to sing a hymn. The others also sang, and their soldiers also joining while standing by the altar.

13 And Eliphaz spoke:
"Taken off is the sin and our injustice is gone
14 But Elihu, the evil one
Will have no memory among the living
His light is darkened and has lost its light

15 The glory of his lamp
Will announce itself for him
For he is the son of darkness
And not of light

16 The doorkeepers of the place of darkness
Will give him their glory and beauty
His Kingdom hath vanished
His throne hath moldered
And the honor of his stature is in Sheol

17 For he has loved the beauty of the serpent
And the skin of the dragon
His gall and his venom
Belong to the Northern One

18 For he did not own himself
Unto Yahuah nor did he fear him
Hut he hated those whom He hath chosen

19 Thus Elohim forgot him
And the holy ones forsook him
His wrath and anger will be unto him desolation
He will have no mercy in his heart nor peace
Because he had the venom of an adder on his tongue

20 Righteous is Yahuah
His judgments are true
With him there is no preference of person
For He judges all alike

21 Behold, Yahuah cometh
Behold, the holy ones have been prepared
The crowns and the prizes of the victors precede them

22 Let the saints rejoice
Let their hearts jump with gladness
They will receive the glory
Which is in store for them.

23 Our sins are forgiven
Our injustice has been cleansed
but Elihu hath no remembrance among the living."

24 After Eliphaz had finished the hymn we rose and went back to the city, each one back to the house where they lived.

25 And the people made a feast for me in thanksgiving and happiness of Elohim, and all my friends came back to me.

26 And all those who had seen me in my former state of happiness, asked me saying: "Who are these three men here with us?"

11

1 But I desired to begin again my work with the poor, so I asked them:

2 "Give each poor person a lamb so they may use it for clothing, and give them each four coins of silver or gold"

3 Then Yahuah blessed all that I had left. After only a few days I became rich again in merchandise, in flocks and all things which I had lost. I received double that which I had lost.

4 Then I also took as wife your mother and became the father of you ten in place of the ten children that had died.

5 And now, my children, having telling you all this, I tell you this one more thing: "I am going to die, and you will take my place.

6 Do not forsake Yahuah. Be loving towards the poor; Do not ignore the weak. Do not marry strange women.

7 Listen, my children, I will divide among you what I own! so that each may have control over his own life and have power to do good with his share of the inheritance."

8 And after Job had spoken, he brought all his goods and divided them among his seven sons. He gave nothing to his daughters.

9 Then they said to their father: "Our adonai and father! Are we not also your children? Why don't you give us a share of your possessions?"

10 Then said Job to his daughters: "Do not become angry, my daughters, I have not forgotten you. Behold, I have saved a possession for you better than that which your brothers have taken."

11 And he called his daughter whose name was Jemima over and talked to her. "Take this double ring used as a key and go to the treasure-house and bring me the golden casket. Then I will give you your inheritance."

12 She went inside and brought it out to him. He opened it and took out three-stringed girdles that were indescribable in all the words of men.

13 They were not an earthly work, but celestial sparks of light flashed through them like the rays of the sun.

14 He gave one string to each of His daughters. He told them: "Put these around you so all the days of your life they may encircle you. They will give you everything good in life."

15 The other daughter Keziah said: "Is this the possession of which you say it is better than that of our brothers? How are we supposed to live on this?"

16 Their father said to them: "These gifts are enough to live on, and they will bring you into a better world to live in. They will give you a life in the heavens.

17 My children, don't you know the value of these things here? Hear then! Yahuah saw that I was worth having mercy on. He took off the plagues and the maggots! He called me and handed to me these three strings!

18 And He said to me: 'Rise and gird up thy loins like a man! I will demand things of you and present yourself to me.'

19 I took them and tied them around my waist. Immediately the maggots fell off my body, and so did the plagues! My whole body took new strength through Yahuah. I was healed, as though I had never suffered in the first place.

20 But also in my heart I forgot the pains. Then Yahuah spoke to me in His great power and showed to me all that was and will be.

21 So children, when you wear these you will not have enemies plot against you. You will also be pure minded because these are charms from Yahuah.

22 Get up and tie these around you before I die in order that you may see the angels come when I leave. Wear them so that you may behold with wonder the powers of Elohim."

23 Then Jemima stood up and tied it around herself and immediately she departed her body. It was her father had said, and she put on another heart, as if she never cared for earthly things.

24 And she sang angelic hymns in the voice of angels, and she chanted forth the angelic praise of Elohim. And she danced.

25 Then the other daughter, Keziah, put on the girdle. Her heart was changed, so that she no longer wished for worldly things.

26 Her mouth spoke the language of the heavenly archons and she sang the hymns of the work of the High Place. If anyone wishes to know the work of the heavens he can read the hymns of Keziah.

27 Then the other daughter Keren Happukh tied it around herself and her mouth spoke in the language of those on high. Her heart was changed - it was lifted above the worldly things.

28 She spoke in the dialect of the Cherubim, singing the praise of the Ruler of the cosmic powers and extolling His glory.

29 And if anyone desires to follow the verses of the "Glory of the Father," they will find them written down in the 'Prayers of Keren Happukh.'

12

1 After these three had finished singing hymns. I, Nahor brother of Job, sit down next to him, as he lay down.

2 And I heard the great things of the three daughters of my brother, one always succeeding the other. After that there was a holy silence.

3 And I wrote down this book containing the hymns except the hymns and signs of The Holy Word. These were the great things of Elohim.

4 And Job lay down from sickness on his couch. But he didn't have any pain or suffering. His pain did not take strong hold of him on account of the charm of the girdle which he had wound around himself.

5 After three days Job saw the holy angels come for his soul. He rose up and took the charm and gave it to his daughter Jemima.

6 And to Keziah he gave a censer with perfume. To Keren Happukh he gave a tambourine in order that they might bless the holy angels who came for his soul.

7 And they took these, and sang, and played on the strings and praised and glorified Elohim in the holy dialect.

8 After all this He came - He who sits upon the great chariot. He kissed Job, while his three daughters looked on, but no one else saw what happened.

9 He took the soul of Job and He soared upward. He took Job's soul by the arm and carrying him upon the chariot, and He went towards the East.

10 Job's body was brought to the grave while the three daughters walked in front. They had put on their charms and they sang hymns in praise of Elohim.

11 His brother Nahor, his seven sons, the people, the poor, the orphans, the feeble, all cried a great song of sadness over him. They sang:

12 "Woe unto us
For today has been taken from us
The strength of the feeble
The light of the blind
The father of the orphans

13 The receiver of strangers
Has been taken off
The leader of the erring
The coverer of the naked
The shield of the widows
Who would not mourn for this man of Elohim?"

14 And as they were singing and crying in all manners and songs, they hesitated in burying him.

15 But then after three days, he was finally put into the grave. He was like a man in sweet slumber. They called his name good and beautiful. His name will remain renowned throughout all the generations of the world.

16 He left behind seven sons and three daughters. There were no daughters found on earth as beautiful as the daughters of Job.

17 The name of Job used to be Jobab, but Yahuah changed his name to Job.

18 Before his plague he lived eighty-five years, and after the plague he doubled that. After the plague he lived 170 years. So he lived a total of 255 years.

19 He saw the sons of his sons to the fourth generation.

It's written that he will rise up with those whom Yahuah will reawaken.

To our Adonai be all the glory.

Amen.

Testament of Job

Original Translation

Testament of Job

the blameless, the sacrifice, the conqueror in many contests.

Book of Job, called Jobab, his life and the transcript of his Testament.

Chapter 1

1 On the day he became sick and (he) knew that he would have to leave his bodily abode, he called his seven sons and his three daughters together and spake to them as follows: 2 "Form a circle around me, children, and hear, and I shall relate to you what the Adonai did for me and all that happened to me. 3 For I am Job your father. 4 Know ye then my children, that you are the generation of a chosen one and take heed of your noble birth.

5 For I am of the sons of Esau. My brother is Nahor, and your mother is Dinah. By her have I become your father. 6 For my first wife died with my other ten children in bitter death. 7 Hear now, children, and I will reveal unto you what happened to me.

8 I was a very rich man living in the East in the land Ausitis, (Utz) and before the Adonai had named me Job, I was called Jobab.

9 The beginning of my trial was thus. 10. Near my house there was the idol of one worshipped by the people; and I saw constantly burnt-offerings brought to him as a elohim.

10 Then I pondered and said to myself: "Is this he who made heaven and earth, the sea and us all How will I know the truth"

11 And in that night as I lay asleep, a voice came and called: "Jobab! Jobab! rise up, and I will tell thee who is the one whom thou wishest to know. 12 This, however, to whom the

people bring burnt-offerings and libations, is not Elohim, but this is the power and work of the Seducer (Satan) by which he beguiles the people".

13 And when I heard this, I fell upon the earth and I prostrated myself saying: 14 "O my Adonai who speakest for the salvation of my soul. I pray thee, if this is the idol of Satan, I pray thee, let me go hence and destroy it and purify this spot. 15 For there is none that can forbid me doing this, as I am the king of this land, so that those that live in it will no longer be led astray".

16 And the voice that spoke out of the flame answered to me: "Thou canst purify this spot. 17. But behold I announce to thee what the Adonai ordered me to tell thee, For I am the archangel of the Elohim". 18 .And I said : "Whatever shall be told to his servant. I shall hear". 19. And the

archangel, said to me : "Thus speaketh the Adonai: If thou undertakest to destroy and takest away the image of Satan, he will set himself with wrath to wage war against thee, and he will display against thee all his malice. 21 He will bring upon thee many severe plagues, and take from thee all that thou hast. 21 He will take away thine children, and will inflict many evils upon thee. 22 Then thou must wrestle like an athlete and resist pain, sure of thy reward, overcome trials and afflictions.

23 But when thou endurest, I shall make thy name renowned throughout all generations of the earth until to the end of the world. 24 And I shall restore thee to all that thou hadst had, and the double part of what thou shalt lose will be given to thee in order that thou mayest know that Elohim does not consider the person but

giveth to each who deserveth the good. 25 And also to thee shall it be given, and thou shalt put on a crown of amarant. 26 And at the resurrection thou shalt awaken for eternal life. Then shalt thou know that he Adonai is just, and true and mighty".

27 Whereupon, my children, I replied: "I shall from love of Elohim endure until death all that will come upon me, and I shall not shrink back". 28 Then the angel put his seal upon me and left me.

Chapter 2

1 After this I rose up in the night and took fifty slaves and went to the temple of the idol and destroyed it to the ground. 2. And so I went back to my house and gave orders that the door should he firmly locked; saying to my doorkeepers : 3 "If somebody shall ask for me, bring no report to me, but tell him : He investigates urgent affairs. He is inside".

4 Then Satan disguised himself as a beggar and knocked heavily at the door, saying to the door-keeper:

5 "Report to Job and say that I desire to meet him",

6 And the door-keeper came in and told me that, but heard from me that I was studying.

7 The Evil One, having failed in this, went away and took upon his shoulder an old, torn basket and went in and spoke to the doorkeeper saying: "Tell Job : Give me bread from thine hands that I may eat". 8 And when I heard this, I gave her burnt bread to give it to him, and I made known to him : "Expect not to eat of my bread, for it is forbidden to thee". 9 But the door-keeper, being ashamed to hand him the burnt and ashy bread, as she did not know that it

was Satan, took of her own fine bread and gave it to him. 10 But he took it and, knowing what occured, said to the maiden : "Go hence, bad servant, and bring me the bread that was given thee to hand to me". 11 And the servant cried and spoke in grief: "Thou speakest the truth, saying that I am a bad servant. because I have not done as I was instructed by my master". 12 And he turned back and brought him the burnt bread and said to him : "Thus says my adonai : Thou shalt not eat of my bread anymore, for it is forbidden to thee. 13 And this he gave me [saying: This I give] in order that the charge may not be brought against me that I did not give to the enemy who asked".) 14 And when Satan heard this, he sent back the servant to me, saying: "As thou seest this bread all burnt, so shall I soon burn thy body to make it like this". 15 And I replied: "Do what thou desirest to do and accomplish whatever thou plottest. For I am ready to endure whatever thou bringest upon me". 16 And when the devil heard this, he left me, and walking up to under the [highest] heaven, he took from the Adonai the oath that he might have power, over all my possessions. 17 And after having taken the power he went and instantly took away all my wealth.

Chapter 3

1 For I had one hundred and thirty thousand sheep, and of these I separated seven thousand for the clothing of orphans and widows and of needy and sick ones. 2 I had a herd of eight hundred dogs who watched my sheep and besides these two hundred to watch my house. 3 And I had nine mills working for the whole city and ships to carry goods, and I seat them into every city and

into the villages to the feeble and sick and to those that were unfortunate. 4 And I had three hundred and forty thousand nomadic asses, and of these I set aside five hundred, and the offspring of these I order to he sold and the proceeds to be given to the poor and the needy. 5 For from all the lands the poor came to meet me.

6 For the four doors of my house were opened, each, being in charge of a watchman who had to see whether there were any people coming asking alms, and whether they would see me sitting at one of the door's so that they could leave through the other and take whatever they needed.

7 I also had thirty immovable tables set at all hours for the strangers alone, and I also had twelve tables spread for the widows. 8 And if any one came asking for alms, he found food on my table to take all he needed, and I turned nobody away to leave my door with an empty stomach.

9 I also had three thousand five hundred yokes of oxen, and I selected of these five hundred and had them tend to the plowing. 10 And with these I had done all the work in each field by those who would, take it in charge and the income of their crops I laid aside for the poor on their table. 11 I also had fifty bakeries from which I sent [the bread] to the table for the poor. 12 And I had slaves selected for their service. 13 There were also some strangers who saw my good will; they wished to serve as waiters themselves. 14 Others, being in distress and unable to obtain a living, came with the request saying: 15 "We pray thee, since we also can fill this office of waiters (deacons) and have no possession, have pity upon us and advance money to us in

order that we may go into the great cities and sell merchandise. 16 And the surplus of our profit we may give as help to the poor, and then shaII we return to thee thine own (money). 17 And when I heard this, I was glad that they should take this altogether from me for the husbandry of charity for the poor. 18 And with a willing heart I gave them what they wanted, and I accepted their written bond, but would not take any other security from them except the written document. 19 And they went abroad and gave to time poor as far as they were successful. 20 Frequently, however, some of their goods were lost on the road or on the sea, or they would he robbed of them. 21 Then they would come and say: "We pray thee, act generously towards us in order that we may see how we can restore to you thine own". 22 And when I heard this, I had sympathy with them, and handed to them their bond, and often having read it before them tore it up and released them of their debt. saying to them : 23 "What I have consecrated for the benefit of the poor, I shall not take from you".

24 And so I accepted nothing from my debtor. 25 And when a man with cheerful heart came to me saying: I am not in need to be compelled to he a paid worker for the poor. 26 But I wish to serve the needy at thy table", and he consented to work, and he ate his share. 27 So I gave him his wages nevertheless, and I went home rejoicing. 28   And when he did not wish to take it, I forced him to do so, saying: "I know that thou art a laboring man who looks for and waits for his wages, and thou must take it."

29 Never did I defer paying the wages of the hireling or any other, nor keep back in

my house for a single evening his hire that was due to him. 30 Those that milked the cows and the ewes signaled to the passersby that they should take their share. 31 For the milk flowed in such plenty that it curdled into butter on the hills and by the road side; and by the rocks and the hills the cattle lay which had given birth to their offspring. 32 For my servants grew weary keeping the meat of the widows and the poor and dividing it into small pieces. 33 For they would curse and say: "Oh that we had of his flesh that we could be satisfied", although I was very kind to them,

34 I also had six harps [and six slaves to play the harps] and also a cithara, a decachord, and I struck it during the day. 35 And I took the cithara, and the widows responded after their meals. 36 And with the musical instrument I reminded them of Elohim that they should give praise to the Adonai. 37 And when my female slaves would murmur, then I took the musical instruments and played as much as they would have done for their wages, and gave them respite from their labor and sighs.

Chapter 4

1 And my children, after having taken charge of the service, took their meals each day along with their three sisters beginning with the older brother, and made a feast.

2 And I rose in the morning and offered as sin-offering for them fifty rams and nineteen sheep, and what remained as a residue was consecrated to the poor. 3 And I said to them : "Take these as residue and pray for my children. 4 Perchance my sons have sinned before the Adonai, speaking in haughtiness of spirit: We are children of

this rich man. Ours are all these goods; why should we be servants of the poor' 5 And speaking thus in a haughty spirit they may have provoked the anger of Elohim, for overbearing pride is an abomination before the Adonai." 6 So I brought oxen as offerings to the priest at the altar saying: "May my children never think evil towards Elohim in their hearts."

7 While I lived in this manner, the Seducer could not bear to see the good [I did], and he demanded the warfare of Elohim against me. 8 And he came upon me cruelly. 9 First he burnt up the large number of sheep, then the camels, then he burnt up the cattle and all my herds; or they were captured not only by enemies but also by such as had received benefits from me. 10 And the shepherds came and announced that to me. 11 But when I heard it, I gave praise to Elohim and did not blaspheme.

12 And when the Seducer learned of my fortitude, he plotted new thing's against me. 13 He disguised himself as King of Persia and besieged my city, and after he had led off all that were therein, he spoke to them in malice, saying in boastful language: 14 "This man Job who has obtained all the goods of the earth and left nothing for others, he has destroyed and torn down the temple of elohim. 15 Therefore shall I repay to him what he has done to the house of the great elohim.

16 Now come with me and we shall pillage all that is left in his house." 17 And they answered and said to him: "He has seven sons and three daughters. 18 Take heed lest they flee into other lands and they may become our tyrants and then come over us with force and kill us." 19 And he said: Be not at all afraid. His flocks and his wealth have I destroyed by fire,

and the rest have I captured, and behold, his children shall I kill." 20 And having spoken thus, he went and threw the house upon my children and killed them. 21 And my fellow-citizens, seeing that what was said by him had become true, came and pursued me, and robbed me of all that was in my house. 22 And I saw with mine own eyes the pillage of my house, and men without culture and without honor sat at my table and on my couches, and I could not remonstrate against them.

23 For I was exhausted like a woman with her loins let loose from multitude of pains, remembering chiefly that this warfare had been predicted to me by the Adonai through His angel. 24 And I became like one who, when seeing the rough sea and the adverse winds, while the lading of the vessel in mid-ocean is too heavy, casts the burden into the sea, saying: 25 "I wish to destroy all this only in order to come safely into the city so that I may take as profit the rescued ship and the best of my things." 26 Thus did I manage my own affairs.

27 But there came another messenger and announced to me the ruin of my own children, and I was shaken with terror. 28 And I tore my clothes and said: The Adonai hath given, the Adonai hath taken. As it hath deemed best to the Adonai, thus it hath come to be. May the name of the Adonai be blessed."

Chapter 5

1 And when Satan saw that he could riot put me to despair, he went and asked my body of the Adonai in order to inflict plague on me, for the Evil one could not bear my patience. 2 Then the Adonai delivered me into his hands to use my body as he wanted, but he gave him no power over

my soul. 3. And he came to me as I was sitting on my throne still mourning over my children. 4 And he resembled a great hurricane and turned over my throne and threw me upon the ground. 5 And I continued lying on the floor for three hours. and he smote me with a hard plague from the top of my head to the toes of my feet. 6 And I left the city in great terror and woe and sat down upon a dunghill my body being worm-eaten. 7 And I wet the earth with the moistness of my sore body, for matter flowed off my body, and many worms covered it. 8 And when a single worm crept off my body, I put it back saying: "Remain on the spot where thou hast been placed until He who hath sent thee will order thee elsewhere."

9 Thus I endured for sever years, sitting on a dung-hill outside of the city while being plague-stricken. 10 And I saw with mine own eyes my longed-for children [carried by angels to heaven] 11 And my humbled wife who had been brought to her bridal chamber in such great luxuriousness and with spearmen as body-guards. I saw her do a water-carrier's work like a slave in the house of a common man in order to win some bread and bring it to me. 12 And in my sore affliction I said: "Oh that these braggart city rulers whom I soul not have thought to be equal with my shepherd dogs should now employ my wife as servant!" 13 And after this I took courage again. 14 Yet afterwards they withheld even the bread that it should only have her own nourishment. 15 But she took it and divided it between herself and me, saying woefully: "Woe to me! Forthwith he may no longer feed on bread, and he cannot go to the market to ask bread of the bread-sellers in order to bring it to me that he may

eat" 16 And when Satan learned this, he took the guise of a bread-seller, and it was as if by chance that my wife met him and asked him for bread thinking that it was that sort of man. 17 But Satan said to her : "Give me the value, and then take what thou wishest." 18 Whereupon she answered saying: Where shall I get money Dost thou not know what misfortune happened to me. If thou hast pity, show it to me; if not, thou shalt see." 19 And he replied saying: "If you did not deserve this misfortune, you would not have suffered all this. 20 Now, if there is no silver piece in thine hand, give me the hair of thine head and take three loaves of bread for it, so that ye may live on there for three days. 21 Then she said to herself: "What is the hair of my head in comparison with my starving husband" 22 And so after having pondered over the matter, she said to

him: "Rise and cut off my hair". 3 Then he took a pair of scissors and took off the hair of her head in the presence of all, and gave her three loaves of bread. 24 Then she took them and brought them to me. And Satan went behind her on the road, hiding himself as he walked and troubling her heart greatly.

Chapter 6

1 And immediately my wife came near me and crying aloud and weeping she said: "Job! Job! How long wilt thou sit upon the dung-hill outside of the city, pondering yet for a while and expecting to obtain your hoped-for salvation!" 2 And I have been wandering from place to place, roaming about as a hired servant, behold they memory has already died away from earth. 3 And my sons and the daughters that I carried on my bosom and the labors and pains that I sustained have been for

nothing 4 And thou sittest in the malodorous state of soreness and worms, passing the nights in the cold air. 5 And I have undergone all trials and troubles and pains, day and night until I succeeded in bringing bread to thee. 6 For your surplus of bread is no longer allowed to me; and as I can scarcely take my own food and divide it between us, I pondered in my heart that it was not right that thou shouldst be in pain and hunger for bread. 7 And so I ventured to go to the market without bashfulness. and when the bread-seller told me: "Give me money. and thou shalt have bread". I disclosed to him our state of distress. 8 Then I heard him say : "If thou hast no money, hand me the hair of thy head, and take three loaves of bread in order that ye may live on these for three days". 9 And I yielded to the wrong and said to him "Rise and cut off my hair !" and he rose and in disgrace cut off with the scissors the hair of my head on the market place while the crowd stood by and wondered. 10 Who would then not be astonished saying: "Is this Sitis, the wife of Job, who had fourteen curtains to cover her inner sitting room, and doors within doors so that he was greatly honored who would be brought near her, and now behold, she barters off her hair for bread!

11 Who had camels laden with goods. and they were brought into remote lands to the poor, and now she sells her hair for bread!

12 Behold her who had seven tables immovably set in her house at which each poor man and each stranger ate, and now she sells her hair for bread!

13 Behold her who had the basin wherewith to wash her feet made of gold and silver, and now she walks

upon the ground and [sells her hair for bread !]

14 Behold her who had her garments made of byssus interwoven with gold, and now she exchanges her hair for bread!

15 Behold her who had couches of gold and of silver, and now she sells her hair for bread!"

16 In short then, Job, after the many things that have been said to me, I now say in one word to thee : 17 "Since the feebleness of my heart has crushed my bones, rise then and take these loaves of bread and enjoy them, and then speak some word against the Adonai and die!

18 For I too, would exchange the torpor of death for the sustenance of my body".

19 But I replied to her "Behold I have been for these seven years plague-stricken, and I have stood the worms of my body, and I was not weighed down in my soul by all these pains. 20 And as to the word which thou sayest: 'Speak some word against Elohim and die!', together with thee I will sustain the evil which thou seest. and let us endure the ruin of all that we have. 21 Yet thou desirest that we should say some word against Elohim and that He should be exchanged for the great Pluto [the elohim of the nether world.] 22 Why dost thou not remember those great goods which we possessed If these goods come from the lands of the Adonai, should not we also endure evils and be high-minded in everything until the Adonai will have mercy again and show pity to us 23 Dost thou not see the Seducer stand behind thee and confound thy thoughts in order that thou shouldst beguile me 24 And he turned to Satan and said : "Why dost thou not come openly to me Stop hiding

thyself thou wretched one, 25 Does the lion show his strength in the weasel cage Or does the bird fly in the basket I now tell thee: Go away and wage thy war against me".

26 Then he went off from behind my wife and placed himself before me crying and he said : Behold, Job, I yield and give way to thee who art but flesh while I am a spirit. 27 Thou art plague-stricken, but I am in great trouble. 28 For I am like a wrestler contesting with a wrestler who has, in a single-handed combat, torn down his antagonist and covered him with dust and broken every limb of his, whereas the other one who lies beneath, having displayed his bravery, gives forth sounds of triumph testifying to his own superior excellence. 29 Thus thou, O Job, art beneath and stricken with plague and pain, and yet thou hast carried the victory in the wrestling-

match with me, and behold, I yield to thee". 30. Then he left me abashed. 31 Now my children, do you also show a firm heart in all the evil that happens to you, for greater than all things is firmness of heart.

Chapter 7

1 At this time the kings heard what had happened to me and they rose and came to me. each from his land to visit me and to comfort me. 2. And when they came near me, they cried with a loud voice and each tore his clothes. 3 And after they had prostrated themselves, touching the earth with their heads, they sat down next to me for seven days and seven nights, and none spoke a word. 4 They were four in numbers: Eliplaz, the king of Teman, and Balad, and Sophar, and Elilhu. 5 And when they had taken their seat, they conversed about what had happened to me. 6 Now when for time first

time they had come to me and I had shown them my precious stones, they were astonished and said : 7 "If of us three kings all our possessions would be brought together into one, it would not come up to the precious stones of .Jobab's kingdom (crown). For thou art of greater nobility than all the people of the East. 8 And when, therefore, they now came to the land of Ausitis "Uz" to visit me, they asked in the city : "Where is Jobab, the ruler of this whole land" 9 And they told them concerning me: "He sitteth upon the dung-hill outside of the city for he has not entered the city' for seven years". 10 And then again they-inquired concerning my possessions, and there was revealed to them all that happened to me. 11 And when they had learned this, they went out of the city with the inhabitants, and my fellow-citizens pointed me out to them. 12 But these remonstrated and said: "Surely, this is not Jobab".

13 And while they hesitated, there said Eliphaz. the King of Teman: "Come let us step near and see." 14 And when they came near I remembered them, and I wept very much when I learned the purpose of their journey. 15 And I threw earth upon my head, and while shaking my head I revealed unto them that I was [Job]. 16 And when they saw me shake my head they threw themselves down upon the ground, all overcome with emotion 17 And while their hosts were standing around, I saw the three kings lie upon the ground for three hours like dead. 18 Then they rose and said to each other: We cannot believe that this is Jobab". 19 And finally, after they had for seven day's inquired after everything concerning me and searched for my flocks and other possessions, they

said: 20 "Do we not know how many goods were sent by him to the cities and the villages round about to be given to the poor, aside from all that was given away by him within his own house How then could he have fallen into such a state of perdition and misery !"

21 And after the seven days Elihu said to the kings : "Come let us step near and examine him accurately, whether he truly is Jobab or not" 22 And they, being not half a mile (stadium) distant from his malodorous body, they rose and stepped near, carrying perfume in their hands, while their soldiers went with them and threw fragrant incense round about them so that they could come near me. 23 And after they had thus passed three hours, covering the way with aroma, they drew nigh. 24 And Eliphaz began and said : "Art thou, indeed, Job, our fellow-king Art thou the one who owned the great glory 25 Art thou he who once shone like the sun of day upon the whole earth Art thou he who once resembled the moon and the stars effulgent throughout the night" 26 And I answered him and said: "I am", and thereupon all wept and lamented, and they sang a royal song of lamentation, their whole army joining them in a chorus.

27 And again Eliphaz said to me : "Art thou he who had ordered seven thousand sheep to be given for the clothing of the poor Whither, then hath gone the glory of thy throne

28 Art thou he who had ordered three thousand cattle to do the plowing of the field for the poor Wither, then hath thy glory gone!

29 Art thou he who had golden couches, and now thou sittest upon a dung

hill [" Whither then hath thy glory gone !"]

30 Art thou he who had sixty tables set for the poor Art thou he who had censer's for the fine perfume made of precious stones, and now thou art in a malodorous state Whither then hath thy glory gone!

31 Art thou he who had golden candelabras set upon silver stands; and now must thou long for the natural gleam of the moon ["Whither then hath thy glory gone !"]

32 Art thou the one who had ointment made of the spices of frankincense, and now thou art in a state of repulsiveness! [Whither then hath thy glory gone !"]

33 Art thou he who laughed the wrong doers and sinners to scorn and now thou hast become a laughingstock to all !" [Whither then hath thine glory gone]

34 And when Eliphaz had for a long time cried and lamented, while all the others joined him, so that the commotion was very great, I said to them : 35 Be silent and I will show you my throne, and the glory of its splendor: My glory will be everlasting. 36 The whole world shall perish, and its glory shall vanish, and all those who hold fast to it, will remain beneath, but my throne is in the upper world and its glory and splendor will be to the right of the Savior in the heavens. 37 My throne exists in the life of the "holy ones" and its glory in the imperishable world. 38 For rivers will he dried up and their arrogance shall go down to the depth of the abyss, but the streams of my land in which my throne is erected, shall not dry up, but shall remain unbroken in strength.

39 The kings perish and the rulers vanish, and their glory and pride is as the

shadow in a looking glass, but my Kingdom lasts forever and ever, and its glory and beauty is in the chariot of my Father).

Chapter 8

I When I spoke thus to them, Ehiphaz. became angry and said to the other friends "For what purpose is it that we have come here with our hosts to comfort him 9 Behold, he upbraids us. Therefore let us return to our countries.

2 This man sits here in misery worm-eaten amidst an unbearable state of putrefaction, and yet he challenges its saving : 'Kingdoms shall perish and their rulers, but my Kingdom, says he, shall last forever'". 3 Eliphaz, then, rose in great commotion, and, turning away from them in great fury, said': "I go hence. We have indeed come to comfort him, but he declares war to us in view of our armies". 4 But then Baldad seized him by the hand and said :" Not thus ought one to speak to an afflicted man, and especially to one stricken down with so many plagues. 5 Behold, we, being in good health, dared not approach him on account of the offensive odor, except with the help of plenty of fragrant aroma. But thou, Eliphaz. art forgetful of all this. 6 Let me speak plainly. Let us be magnanimous and learn what is the cause Must he in remembering his former days of happiness not become mad in his mind 7 Who should not be altogether perplexed seeing himself thus lapse into misfortune and plagues But let me step near him that I may find by what cause is he thus" 9 And Baldad rose and approached me saying: "Art thou Job" and he said : "Is thy heart still in good keeping 9 And I said: "I did not hold fast to the earthly things, since the earth with all that inhabit it is unstable. But my heart

holds fast to the heaven, because there is no trouble in heaven".

10 Then Baldad rejoined and said : "We know that the earth is unstable, for it changes according to season. At times it is in a state of peace, and at times it is in a state of war. But of the heaven we hear that it is perfectly steady. 11 But art thou truly in a state of calmness Therefore let me ask and speak, and when thou answerest me to my first word, I shall have a second question to ask, and if again thou answerest in well-set words, it will be manifest that thy heart has not been unbalanced". 12 And I said : "Upon what dost thou set thy hope" And I said: "Upon the living Elohim". 13. And he said to me : "Who deprived thee of all thou didst possess And who inflicted thee with these plagues 9" And I said: "Elohim". 14 And he said: "If thou still placest thy hope upon Elohim, how can He do wrong in judgment, having brought upon thee these plagues and misfortunes, and having taken from thee all thy possessions 15 And since He has taken these, it is clear that He has given thee nothing. No king will disgrace his soldier who has served him well as body-guard" 16 [And I answered saying] : "Who understands the depths of the Adonai and of His wisdom to be able to accuse Elohim of injustice" 17 [And Baldad said] : "Answer me, o Job, to this. Again I say to thee : 'If thou art in a state of calm reason, teach me if thou hast wisdom: 18 Why do we see the sun rise in the East and set in the West And again when rising in the morning we find him rise in the East Tell me thy-thought about this" 19 Then said I: "Why shall I betray (babble forth) the mighty mysteries of Elohim And should my mouth stumble in revealing things belonging to the Master

Never! 20 Who are we that we should pry into matters concerning the upper world while we are only of flesh, nay, earth and ashes! 21 In order that you know that my heart is sound, hear what I ask you: 22 Through the stomach cometh food, and water you drink through the mouth, and then it flows through the same throat, and when the two go down to become excrement, they again part; who effects this separation". 23 And Baldad said: "I do not know". And I rejoined and said to him : "If thou dost not understand even the exits of the body, how canst thou understand the celestial circuits"

24 Then Sophar rejoined and said : "We do not inquire after our own affairs, but we desire to know whether thou art in a sound state, and behold, we see that thy reason has not been shaken. 25. What now dost thou wish that we should do for thee Behold, we have come here and brought the physicians of three kings, and if thou wishest, thou mayest he cured by them". 26 But I answered and said : "My cure and my restoration cometh from Elohim, the Maker of physicians".

Chapter 9

1 And when I spoke thus to them, behold, there my wife Sitis came running, dressed in rags. from the service of the master by whom she was employed as slave though she had been forbidden to leave, lest the kings, on seeing her, might take her as captive. 2 And when she came, she threw herself prostrate to their feet, crying and saying: ''Remember'. Eliphaz and ye other friends, what I was once with you, and how I have changed, how I am now dressed to meet you" 3 Then the kings broke forth in great weeping and, being in double perplexity, they

kept silent. But Eliphaz took his purple mantle and cast it about her to wrap herself up with it. 4 But she asked him saying: "I ask as favor of you, my Lords, that you order your soldiers that they should dig among the ruins of our house which fell upon my children, so that their bones could be brought in a perfect state to the tombs. 5 Fir as we have, owing to our misfortune, no power at all, and so we may at least see their bones. 6 For have I like a brute the motherly feeling of wild beasts that my ten children should have perished on one day and not to one of them could I give a decent burial" 7 And the kings gave order that the ruins of my house should be dug up. But I prohibited it, saving 8 "Do not go to the trouble in vain; for my children will not he found, for they are in the keeping of their Maker and Ruler".

9 And the kings answered and said : "Who will gainsay that he is out of his mind and raves 10 For while we desire to bring the bones of his children back, he forbids us to do so saying: 'They have been taken and placed the keeping of their Maker'. Therefore prove unto us the truth". 11 But I said to them: "Raise me that I may stand up, and they lifted me, holding up my arms from both sides. 12 And I stood upright, and pronounced first the praise of Elohim and after the prayer I said to them : "Look with your eyes to the East". 13 And they looked and saw my children with crowns near the glory of the King, the Ruler of heaven.

14 And when my wife Sitis saw this, she fell to the ground and prostrated [herself] before Elohim, saying: "Now I know that my memory remains with the Adonai". 15 And after

she had spoken this, and the evening came, she went to the city, back to the master whom she served as slave, and lay herself down at the manger of the cattle and died there from exhaustion. 16 And when her despotic master searched for her and did not find her, he came to the fold of his herds, and there he saw her stretched out upon the manger dead, while all the animals around were crying about her. 17 And all who saw her wept and lamented, and the cry extended throughout the whole city. 18 And the people brought her down and wrapt her up and buried her by the house which had fallen upon her children. 19 And the poor of the city made a great mourning for her and said: "Behold this Sitis whose like in nobility and in glory is not found in any woman. Alas ! she was not found worthy of a proper tomb!" 20 The dirge for her you will find in the record.

Chapter 10

But Eliphaz and those that were with him were astonished at these things, and they sat down with me and replying to me, spoke in boastful words concerning me for twenty seven days. 2 They repeated it again and again that I suffered deservedly thus for having committed many sins, and that there was no hope left for me, but I retorted to these men in zest of contention myself. 3 And they rose in anger, ready to part in wrathful spirit. But Elihu conjured them to stay yet a little while until he would have shown them what it was. 4 "For", said he, "so many days did you pass, allowing Job to boast that he is just. But I shall no longer suffer it. 5 For from the beginning did I continue crying over him, remembering his former happiness. But now he speaks boastfully and in overbearing pride he says that he has his throne in the heavens. 6 Therefore, hear me, and I will tell you what is the cause of his destiny. 7 Then, imbued with the spirit of Satan. Elihu spoke hard words which are written down in the records left of Elihu. 8 And after he had ended, Elohim appeared to me in a storm and in clouds, and spoke. blaming Elihu and showing me that he who had spoken was not a man, but a wild beast.

9 And when Elohim had finished speaking to me, the Adonai spoke to Eliphaz: "Thou and thy friends have sinned in that ye have not spoken the truth concerning my servant Job. 10 Therefore rise up and make him bring a sin-offering for you in order that your sins may be forgiven; for were it not for him, I would have destroyed you". 11 And so they brought to me all that belonged to a sacrifice, and I took it and brought for them a sin-offering, and the Adonai received it favorably and forgave them their wrong. 12 Then when Eliphaz, Baldad and Sophar saw that Elohim had graciously pardoned their sin through His servant Job, but that He did not deign to pardon Elihu, then did Eliphaz begin to sing a hymn, while the others responded, their soldiers also joining while standing by the altar. 13 And Eliphaz spoke thus

"Taken off is the sin

and our injustice gone;

14 But Elihu, the evil one, shall have no remembrance among the living; his luminary is extinguished and has lost its light.

15 The glory of his lamp will announce itself for him, for he is the son of darkness. and not of light.

16 The doorkeepers of the place of darkness shall give him their glory and beauty as share; His Kingdom hath

vanished, his throne hath moldered, and the honor of his stature is in (Sheol) Hades.

17 For he has loved the beauty of the serpent and the scales (skins) of' the dracon his gall and his venom belongs to the Northern One (Zphuni = Adder).

18 For he did not own himself unto the Adonai nor did he fear him, but he hated those whom He hath chosen (known).

19 Thus Elohim forgot him, and "the holy ones" forsook him, his wrath and anger shall be unto him desolation and he will have no mercy in his heart nor peace, because he, had the venom of an adder on his tongue.

20 Righteous is the Adonai, and His judgments are true, With him there is no preference of person, for He judgeth all alike.

21 Behold, the Adonai cometh! Behold, the "holy ones" have been prepared: The crowns and the prizes of the victors precede them!

22 Let the saints rejoice, and let their hearts exult in gladness; for they shall receive the glory which is in store for them.

Chorus.

23 Our sins are forgiven, our injustice has been cleansed, but Elihu hath no remembrance among the living".

24 After Eliphaz had finished the hymn, we rose and went back to the city, each to the house where they lived.

25 And the people made a feast for me in gratitude and delight of Elohim, and all my friends came back to me.

26 And all those who had seen me in my former state of happiness, asked me

saying: "What are those three things here amongst us"

Chapter 11

1 But I being desirous to take up again my work of benevolence for the poor, asked them saying: 2 "Give me each a lamb for the clothing of the poor in their state of nakedness, and four drachmas (coins) of silver or gold" 3 Then the Adonai blessed all that was left to me, and after a few days I became rich again in merchandise, in flocks and all things which I had lost, and I received all in double number again. 4 Then I also took as wife your mother and became the father of you ten in place of the ten children that had died.

5 And now, my children, let me admonish you: "Behold I die. You will take my place.

6 Only do not forsake the Adonai. Be charitable towards the poor; Do not disregard the feeble. Take not unto yourselves wives from strangers.

7 Behold, my children, I shall divide among you what I possess, so that each may have control over his own and have full power to do good with his share". 8 And after he had spoken thus, he brought all his goods and divided them among his seven sons, but he gave nothing of his goods to his daughters.

9 Then they said to their father: "Our adonai and father! Are we not also thy children Why, then, dost thou not also give us a share of thy possessions" 10 Then said Job to his daughters : "Do not become angry my daughters. I have not forgotten you. Behold, I have preserved for you a possession better than that which your brothers have taken". 11 And he called his daughter whose name was Day (Yemima) and said to

her: "Take this double ring used as a key and go to the treasure-house and bring me the golden casket, that I may give you your possession". 12 And she went and brought it to him, and he opened it and took out three-stringed girdles about the appearance of which no man can speak. 13 For they were not earthly work, but celestial sparks of light flashed through them like the rays of the sun. 14 And he gave one string to each of His daughters and said: "Put these as girdles around you in order that all the days of your life they may encircle you and endow you with every thing good".

15 And the other daughter whose name was Kassiah said: "Is this the possession of which thou sayest it is better than that of our brothers What now Can we live on this" 16 And their father said to them: "Not only have you here sufficient to live on, but these bring you into a better world to live in, in the heavens. 17 Or do you not know my children, the value of these things here Hear then! When the Adonai had deemed me worthy to have compassion on me and to take off my body the plagues and the worms, He called me and handed to me these three strings. 15 And He said to me: 'Rise and gird up thy loins like a man I will demand of thee and declare thou unto me'. 19 And I took them and girt them around my loins, and immediately did the worms leave my body, and likewise did the plagues, and my whole body took new strength through the Adonai, and thus I passed on, as though I had never suffered. 20 But also in my heart I forgot the pains. Then spoke the Adonai unto me in His great power and showed to me all that was and will be.

21 Now then, my children, in keeping these, you will not have the enemy plotting against you nor [evil] intentions in your mind because this is a charm (Phylacterion) from the Adonai. 22 Rise then and gird these around you before I die in order that you may see the angels come at my parting so that you may behold with wonder the powers of Elohim". 23 Then rose the one whose name was Day (Yemima) and girt herself; and immediately she departed her body, as her father had said, and she put on another heart, as if she never cared for earthly things. 24 And she sang angelic hymns in the voice of angels, and she chanted forth the angelic praise of Elohim while dancing.

25 Then the other daughter, Kassia by name, put on the girdle, and her heart was transformed, so that she no longer wished for worldly things. 26 And her mouth assumed the dialect of the heavenly rulers (Archonts) and she sang the donology of the work of the High Place and if any one wishes to know the work of the heavens he may take an insight into the hymns of Kassia.

27 Then did the other daughter by the name of Amalthea's Horn (Keren Happukh) gird herself and her mouth spoke in the language of those on high; for her heart was transformed, being lifted above the worldly things. 28 She spoke in the dialect of the Cherubim, singing the praise of the Ruler of the cosmic powers (virtues) and extolling their (His) glory.

29 And he who desires to follow the vestiges of the "Glory of the Father" will find them written down in the Prayers of Amalthea's Horn.

Chapter 12

1 After these three had finished singing hymns. did I Nahor (Neros) brother of Job sit down next to him, as he lay down. 2 And I heard the marvelous (great) things of the three daughters of my brother, one always succeeding the other amidst awful silence. 3 And I wrote down this book containing the hymns except the hymns and signs of the [holy] Word, for these were the great things of Elohim. 4 And Job lay down from sickness on his couch, yet without pain and suffering, because his pain did not take strong hold of him on account of, the charm of the girdle which he had wound around himself. 5 But after three days Job saw the holy angels come for his soul, and instantly he rose and took the cithara and gave it to his daughter Day (Yemima). 6 And to Kassia he gave a censer (with perfume = Kassia, and to Amalthea's horn (= music) he gave a timbrel in order that they might bless the holy angels who came for his soul.

7 And they took these, and sang, and played on the psaltery and praised and glorified Elohim in the holy dialect.

8 And after this he came He who sitteth upon the great chariot and kissed Job, while his three daughters looked on, but the others saw it not. 9 And He took the soul of Job and He soared upward, taking her (the soul) by the arm and carrying her upon the chariot, and He went towards the East. 10 His body, however, was brought to the grave while the three daughters marched ahead, having put on their girdles and singing hymns in praise of Elohim.

11 Then held Nahor (Nereos) his brother and his seven sons, with the rest of the people and the poor, the orphans and the feeble

ones, a great mourning over him, saying:

12 "Woe unto us, for today has been taken from us the strength of the feeble, the light of the blind, the father of the orphans;

13 The receiver of strangers has been taken off the leader of the erring, the cover of the naked. the shield of the widows. Who would not mourn for the man of Elohim! 14 And as they were mourning in this and in that form, they would not suffer him to be put into the grave. 15 After three days, however, he was finally put into the grave, like one in sweet slumber, and he received the name of the good (beautiful) who will remain renowned throughout all generations of the world.

16 He left seven sons and three daughters, and there were no daughters found on earth as fair as the daughters of Job. 17 The name of Job was formerly Jobab, and he was called Job by the Adonai. 18 He had lived before his plague eighty five years, and after the plague he took the double share of all; hence also his year's he doubled, which is 170 years. Thus he lived altogether 255 years. 19 And, he saw sons of his sons unto the fourth generation. It is written that he will rise up with those whom the Adonai will reawaken. To our Adonai by glory. Amen.

Printed in Great Britain
by Amazon

21493075R00051